IMPERMANENT WAY

THE CLOSED RAILWAY LINES OF BRITAIN
VOLUME 15

ACROSS THE SHIRES
With a feature on North West Motive Power Depots 1968

Jeffery Grayer
www.crecy.co.uk

© 2020 Jeffery Grayer

ISBN 9781909328969

First published 2020 by Noodle Books
An imprint of Crécy Publishing Ltd

A CIP record for this book is available from the British Library

Printed in Malta by Melita Press

Noodle Books is an imprint of
Crécy Publishing Limited
1a Ringway Trading Estate
Shadowmoss Road
Manchester M22 5LH

www.crecy.co.uk

Publisher's note: Every effort has been made to identify and correctly attribute photographic credits. Any error that may have occurred is entirely unintentional. All uncredited photographs are by the author

Front cover The forlorn remains of Adderbury station on the former line between Banbury and Cheltenham lie deserted and abandoned. Passenger services had been withdrawn from the station in 1951 although freight continued to pass through until complete closure came in 1969.

Rear cover Brackley in Northamptonshire boasted two stations, like many communities that came to be served by the former Great Central Railway (GCR). This is the London and North Western (LNWR) station from which passenger services had been withdrawn in January 1961, as the GCR services from Brackley Central proved to be more attractive and drained much traffic from the Banbury–Verney Junction route. Goods traffic lasted for a further three years.

Frontispiece Cattle now graze in the cutting near Musgrave on the former Eden Valley route between Penrith and Kirkby Stephen East, which closed to passengers in November 1952.

Opposite Stalybridge station is still operational, although the signage seen here has been modernised. The service from Stalybridge to Stockport has, since 1992, achieved fame amongst the railway fraternity, being operated just once a week in each direction. This minimal service, termed a parliamentary train for historical reasons, avoids the official procedures of terminating a passenger service and it has been claimed that the cost of operating this one train would be cheaper than the cost of the closure procedure. The station buffet seen here has also proved popular with railway and real ale enthusiasts.

CONTENTS

INTRODUCTION

Above The shafts of light penetrating the stygian gloom of the interior of a locomotive shed, giving rise to the oft-quoted comparison of a motive power depot to a 'cathedral of steam', is well demonstrated in this view of Manchester's Newton Heath shed, seen here in July 1968 just days before the demise of steam on BR.

This volume, which has now grown to number fifteen in the series, is something of a departure from the previous books in that it does not look at disused lines and stations from one or two specific counties, but instead crosses the country from the South Coast to the Scottish Highlands in more than 170 images. We also examine some of the wider aspects of railway infrastructure, including signal boxes, such as the unusual former platform-mounted signal box at Amberley, and steam motive power depots, along with a brief look at the scene in the North West in 1968, the final year of BR's steam operations. Several of the locations have been showcased in previous volumes but none of the views in this current volume have featured before. One or two routes, such as Bristol–Severn Beach, Ashford–Hastings and the Settle–Carlisle line, which are still operational, also feature as they fell under the threat of closure at one time and today's view of these now 'basic railways' is very different from those of fifty years ago.

It is pleasing to report that some locations, such as Kirkby Stephen East, Lakeside, Alston and Market Bosworth, once deemed irretrievably lost, have been resurrected under the auspices of preservation groups. Perhaps the most significant of the BR re-openings featured here has been Birmingham's Snow Hill station which, although on nothing like the grand scale of its previous incarnation, is now busy with commuters. Similarly, other BR success stories have included Kenilworth and Bicester Village, formerly London Road, re-opened in a modern guise in an attempt to undo what, with the benefit of hindsight, were the somewhat short-sighted closure policies of the past.

Jeffery Grayer
Devon, 2020

HAMPSHIRE & ISLE OF WIGHT

Right Southampton Terminus closed on 5 September 1966 and the first of two views of this impressive terminus shows the ornate facade which formerly carried beneath the clock a signboard stating 'Southampton Docks Station', which was latterly altered to 'Southampton Terminus' in 1935. The main station building, Grade II listed and designed by Sir William Tite, now does duty as a casino.

Right This platform view, taken in 1968, illustrates the growth of vegetation on the redundant tracks since closure. The platforms would be rather ignominiously removed and the area became a car park before much of it was later redeveloped for housing.

The former steam shed at Bournemouth Central lies empty and trackless following the end of steam services on the Southern Region (SR) in July 1967. The new traction in the form of the electric multiple unit (EMU) seen here now rules the roost to London, whilst diesel power takes services on to Weymouth. It would not be until 1988 that electrification was extended westwards to Weymouth.

Right Vegetation has overtaken the platform at Mill Hill on the southern outskirts of Cowes. This was a stop that was particularly well used by workers at the shipyards in Cowes. The line from Cowes to Ryde closed on 21 February 1966. The site of the station now forms a small park, named Arctic Park, and the mouth of the 208-yard tunnel seen here has been blocked up.

Right Bordon Longmoor Military Railway (LMR) signal box, or more correctly block post as the army termed them, is seen through the mouldering remains of the substantial station layout. The LMR made connection here with the BR branch from Bentley which closed to goods traffic in April 1966, but this connection did not long survive the closure of the BR branch, the LMR route being cut back to nearby Oakhanger which served the garrison at Bordon Camp, shortly afterwards.

An exterior view of the attractive station at Tisted on the Meon Valley route – which closed on 7 February 1955 – is enhanced by a dusting of snow in this late 1960s image. This elevation of the station is now screened from the road by a hedge and trees following its conversion into a private dwelling.

Right Similar wintry weather graces this view of Privett station, also on the former Meon Valley route from Fareham to Alton. A fish pond occupies the space between the platforms in this 1960s view, although today the area has been lawned over.

Right Farringdon continued to handle goods traffic after closure of the Meon Valley route but is seen here following track removal in 1970 – although the heaps of coal lying around would suggest that the area was still being used by local merchants. The substantial goods shed is seen on the right and after removal of the passenger platform a new concrete loading dock, also seen here, was built to handle bulk materials such as sugar beet. Aylwards Mill is prominent in the background. The site is now a small industrial park.

Left Three views of Butts Junction where the Meon Valley route met the Alton–Winchester and Alton–Basingstoke lines to the west of Alton. In the first image an express headed by Merchant Navy Pacific No 35008 *Orient Line* forges westwards with the 10:30 Waterloo–Weymouth service on 15 May 1966 diverted to run 'over the Alps', as the gradients on the Winchester route were known, in connection with electrification engineering work on the former London & South Western Railway (LSWR) mainline. Note the grindstone between the diverging tracks used by permanent way men for sharpening tools and scythes when keeping lineside vegetation under control. The stub of the former Meon Valley route to Farringdon can be seen on the left.

Left The second view, looking in the opposite direction towards Alton, sees a two-car Hampshire diesel-electric multiple unit (DEMU) No 1121 heading towards Winchester on 1 May 1966 with the 11:09 Alton–Southampton service. Until closure in 1967 access to the remnant of the former line to Basingstoke, which also diverged here and served Treloar's Hospital, was controlled by a ground frame.

Left The final view, taken from a Winchester-bound DEMU service, shows that the grass-grown track to Farringdon has been disused for some time. The Winchester route was itself to close in February 1973. The trackside grindstone is still in situ but by the look of the lineside vegetation is not often used!

Shawford Junction was where the Didcot, Newbury & Southampton (DN&S) line joined the main LSWR route to Southampton and these two views, taken in early 1967, illustrate the removal of the track and signals which formerly controlled the junction. In the first view an unidentified Bulleid Pacific in original condition sweeps past a lone railwayman standing at the lineside with a Bournemouth-bound service. The track to the right from which the rails have been removed was laid in 1943 to form a link between the down Winchester Chesil branch road and the mainline south of Shawford station, thus keeping DN&S trains from conflicting with movements on the down LSWR mainline at the junction. In the second view a northbound service hauled by a Standard Class 5 is about to pass a junction signal post which has already had its arms removed. The signal box here had closed in November 1966.

Winchester Chesil seen in its death throes in 1965. Although the track remains in position, it is very rusty and has not seen any regular rail movement for some months. The platform is crumbling but the signalling remains in place. Track was removed in the vicinity of the tunnel in the autumn of 1966 and the station building later levelled.

Two further views of Chesil, this time following track removal, looking south from inside the 441-yard tunnel under Winchester's St Giles Hill and north from the angled footbridge which, refurbished, still crosses the route of the old line today. The site of the station is now occupied by a multi-storey car park.

Sutton Scotney's brick-built, rather utilitarian signal box was one of those put in to control wartime traffic and to increase the line's capacity in 1943. The tablet exchange apparatus pole is still standing, as is the signalman's former concrete 'privy' adjacent to the box.

Right The rotting remains of Langstone Bridge serving the former Hayling Island branch, which closed in November 1963, are seen shortly before demolition in 1966.

Right Horsebridge was one of the intermediate stops on the Romsey–Andover line which was closed in September 1964. This view, taken from north of the station, seen in the distance, shows a former bridge over the Park Stream, a tributary of the meandering River Test, which the line followed for much of its length.

Left Longparish on the spur from Fullerton Junction to Hurstbourne, which was something of a white elephant, was an early passenger casualty, being closed in July 1931. It continued to handle goods traffic, however, until May 1956, serving extensive RAF ammunition stores.

Left All that was left of Andover Town station by the time this 1970s view was taken was a set of crossing gates which formerly protected the line where it crossed the busy Bridge Street en route to Andover Junction station. Andover's multi-storey telephone exchange can be seen in the right background.

SUSSEX

Above The two villages after which the station was named 'Rogate for Harting' were 1½ miles away respectively, the station serving the local population of Nyewood. The Petersfield–Midhurst line closed completely in February 1955, with track being lifted at Rogate in December 1957. This view shows that the platform and station building remained in situ after closure, although a newly installed concrete sectional garage does nothing to enhance the view.

Right Midhurst Tunnel seen from the east end during the period when goods traffic was still handled via the route to Pulborough. The permanent way looks to be in fine fettle but total closure came to Midhurst's railway in October 1964.

Left Petworth seen during its nadir with vegetation threatening to overwhelm the wooden station building and platform. Fortunately, the station was saved and now does duty as a luxury B&B establishment complete with Pullman cars.

Below Two views taken in April 1985 of an increasingly decrepit Fittleworth, with the platform canopy, which appears to be sheltering a variety of building materials, having to be supported from imminent collapse. This building has also been saved and was converted to residential use in 1987.

Right West Grinstead, on the line from Shoreham to Horsham, had unusually its main station building and stationmaster's house situated at road level – considerably higher than the platforms, which can be seen lower left in this view. Closed in March 1966, the station building is boarded up and would later be demolished. The trackbed here now forms part of the Downs Link and a carriage on a short length of rail now acts as an Information Office for this facility.

Below Prior to complete demolition and replacement with a modern utilitarian structure, the former grandiose station at Christ's Hospital, junction of the two branchlines to Guildford and Shoreham, is starting to look rather neglected. Looking towards the south signal box, seen in the distance, it is apparent that the track of the little-used down loop line has been removed and would later be infilled. As a temporary measure, a plank appears to have been placed to bridge the gap.

A trio of images of Amberley on the Mid Sussex route taken in July 1985. An interesting feature of this station, which is still open to traffic, was the platform-mounted signal box seen in operation in these views with the signalman in attendance. Built in 1934 the box contained fourteen levers but was closed in March 2014 and has since been gutted, although the cabin remains in situ.

Right Another station which remains open although only as a shadow of its former self is Winchelsea on the Ashford–Hastings line. It is seen here in the late 1960s, when the station building was still in railway ownership, along with the traditional level crossing gates, semaphore signalling and green enamel signage. A lone passenger waits for the next service to Hastings at one of the staggered platforms. Today just the Ashford platform survives alongside a single track, although the former station building seen here is still extant.

Right Eridge signal box is seen on 6 July 1985, the last day of services to Tunbridge Wells. A DEMU No 1311, suitably adorned with headboard carrying the message 'The Groombridge Line 1866-1985', is about to enter the station. Today the Spa Valley Railway once again provides services from Tunbridge Wells West to Eridge. The signal box has been left in situ by Network Rail for future use by the preservation society but is currently boarded up. Just one of the four former platforms at Eridge now sees trains to and from Uckfield, whilst the Spa Valley Railway uses platforms 2 and 3.

SURREY

Left Seen from a passing DEMU en route from Tonbridge in the spring of 1969, the former Motive Power Depot at Redhill is seemingly devoid of occupants. However, close inspection reveals that lurking inside is a steam locomotive in the shape of Standard Pacific No 70000 *Britannia*. Initially it was planned that *Britannia* would form part of the National Collection but in the event the National Railway Museum chose to preserve No 70013 *Oliver Cromwell* instead. Following withdrawal, the locomotive was stored firstly at Stratford, then at Preston Park Pullman Car Works in Brighton and subsequently at Redhill. During this time the East Anglian Locomotive Preservation Society was formed and bought No 70000 in 1970 after which it was moved to the Severn Valley Railway in April 1971, where it was eventually returned to steam in May 1978.

Left Baynards station on the Horsham–Guildford branch lost its passenger service on 14 June 1965. Although the signal box has gone in this mid-1970s view along with the level crossing gates, now replaced with wooden fencing, the station appears pretty intact and the main building survives to this day.

SOMERSET

The Clevedon branch in North Somerset continued to provide a useful service for commuters to Bristol until withdrawal on 3 October 1966. Even the introduction of diesel traction from 1960 was unable to halt eventual closure. A green-liveried single car with 'speed whiskers' is seen here in the summer of 1964 at the terminus prior to returning to the mainline junction at Yatton.

Left The crew of a two-car diesel multiple unit (DMU) await departure from Clevedon in 1963. Today residents of the town no doubt wish their traffic-choked journey into Bristol could be avoided by using the train.

Left This sad scene of demolition took place in 1968. Both the overall roof and the station building, which was rebuilt in 1890, were swept away and replaced by a small shopping centre.

BRISTOL AREA

A scene of yesteryear, when wagonload freight traffic was still important to the railways, is revealed in this panorama of Bristol East Depot as a Class 50 powers past with a parcels train. Coal wagons are evident on the left whilst numerous wagons and vans adorn the many sidings of the up yard. Today the scene is utterly transformed, with the majority of the sidings in the up yard having been removed and much of the site becoming an industrial estate. Bristol East Depot was opened in 1890 to cater for extra traffic brought about by the opening of the Severn Tunnel. The down yard remained in use as storage for engineering wagons before being lifted at the end of 2004. The following year new sidings were laid on the site of the down yard and the Bristol Steel Terminal opened at a cost of £400,000.

Left Tunnelling under Redcliffe Hill was one of the formerly extensive series of lines which served Bristol Docks. Steps leading up to a now non-existent footbridge remain in place, although the steam-powered bascule bridge crossing part of the docks known as Bathurst Basin, seen in the foreground, has been removed. Redcliffe Tunnel, at 292 yards in length, led on to Redcliffe Viaduct, which was adjacent to Temple Meads station, to the east of which the docks line made a connection with the mainline network. In the other direction, after serving the Floating Harbour, the line swung round over the Ashton swing bridge to join the Portishead branch at Ashton Junction and thence to the mainline outside Parson Street station. The connection from Temple Meads closed in 1964, although the steam engine from the bascule bridge is now preserved in Bristol Industrial Museum. A pedestrian footbridge replaces the former bascule bridge today.

Left The Canons Marsh branch closed the following year, with part of the Canons Marsh goods sheds now being the home of We The Curious, a hands-on science and art centre. Some of the goods sheds are seen in the background to this view, which prominently features a most unusual ladies' convenience in the shape of a former trolleybus which was an ex-Portsmouth Corporation AEC/EE/Cravens vehicle reg no RV9109, which had been withdrawn in 1952 and stored until sold to the City of Bristol Transport & Cleansing Department in 1957 and then converted to a mobile ladies' convenience.

Although reduced to single track, Redland station, opened in 1897 on the Clifton Extension Railway, still has much to admire in this early 1970s image. The platform buildings, booking office (seen top right), footbridge and vintage signage all add to the charm of this view. The down track was lifted in October 1970 followed by demolition of the down side shelter, footbridge and ticket office in 1973. The main building on the up platform remains today, but no longer in railway use.

Opposite below The next station on Bristol's sole remaining inner branchline is at Clifton Down seen here with another single car en route to Severn Beach. The buildings were, in their day, described as 'commodious and handsome', being built in a modified Gothic style with long curving platforms covered for much of their length with a glass ridge and furrow roof, the remnants of which are still evident in this late 1960s view. Total removal of these canopies came in May 1971. This was the nearest station for Bristol Zoo and many excursions in connection with this attraction were run in past years. The station became unstaffed in July 1967.

Left A wintry scene sees the passage of a single-car DMU between Redland and Clifton Down. Such single cars were sufficient to cope with traffic outside peak times.

Right As an aside, this is the facade of the lower terminus of the Clifton Rocks Railway, which has been shored up with some ungainly concrete pillars. Closure in 1934 did not mean the end of a useful life for this 500ft-long inclined tunnel leading up to the top of the Clifton Gorge adjacent to the Clifton Gorge Hotel and Brunel's famous suspension bridge, as the BBC took it over during the Second World War as a secret transmission base. The Clifton Rocks Railway Trust is currently working to restore parts of this historic structure.

This view shows the site of the once extensive goods yard of Clifton Down to the right with coal being the principal commodity, as witnessed by the remaining sleeper-built coal pens. The signal box seen at the western end of the platform had a twenty-eight-lever frame and continued in operation until November 1970 when the route was largely singled, although a double track loop was retained through the station here and so it remains today. A shopping centre and car park now cover the former goods yard.

Right Two single cars cross the bridge over the River Trym where the remains of a dock wall at Sea Mills can be seen. In 1712, Joshua Franklyn, a Bristol merchant, built a wet dock at Sea Mills to eliminate the need for large sailing ships to navigate the dangerous River Avon any further upstream, but poor onward transport links doomed the enterprise and the harbour facilities had fallen into disrepair by the end of the 18th century. Sea Mills was once the site of a Roman settlement named Portus Abonae.

Right Avonmouth Dock station plays host to a single-car DMU which is about to leave under semaphore signalling and negotiate the level crossing just to the west of the footbridge seen in the distance. The building on the down platform to the left was later demolished, although the up platform still retains the waiting shelter seen in this view. The imposing white building in the background is a flour mill.

Above The former ticket collector's wooden cabin at the exit from the platform retains its antiquated signage with pointing hand in this view, although it looks to be on its last legs.

Above Seen through a tangle of broken wire fencing, St Andrews Road retains its old running in board, which is seen against a backdrop of shipping tied up at the dockside.

Left A low evening sun illuminates Holesworth Junction signalbox, which controlled entry to a large collection of dock sidings near St Andrews Road. Dating from 1941, being a replacement for a 1910 box destroyed in an air raid, this box closed on 25 January 1988. It is seen here overseeing the passage of a single DMU heading to Severn Beach.

Right Three views of the railway at Bedminster, the first station out of Bristol Temple Meads en route to Exeter. This subway entrance sported an overhead sign with cut out letters formerly illuminated from within advertising the fact that this was 'Bedminster Station'. The station became unstaffed in September 1968 prior to which the platforms became devoid of buildings, although glass and metal bus shelters were subsequently erected. Passenger usage was recorded as 91,822 in 2017/18.

Below Seen from the adjacent Victoria Park, which affords an excellent view of the railway here, is a Hymek-powered van train which can be seen trundling through the lengthy platforms which still carried a period running in board in the late 1960s.

Below Also viewed from the park are unidentified Warship and Hymek diesels coupled together on this multi-tracked section of route from nearby Temple Meads.

BERKSHIRE

Part of the platform at Hermitage station on the former route from Didcot to Newbury, which closed in September 1962, has been demolished in this view. The station house remains in use today by a scaffolding company and residential development has subsequently occurred on the site of the former goods yard.

Right A scene of devastation at Hampstead Norris, where only the platform and goods loading dock remain in this view. A road named Station Hill is the sole testament today to the former presence of a railway here.

Right There was never much to see at lonely Churn halt, situated in a remote spot on the Berkshire Downs. The crumbling platform seen here only ever sported a small waiting shelter, the provision of a halt here being intended as temporary to accommodate a competition held by the National Rifle Association in 1888. However, from 1889 military summer camps were established near to the station so the halt became a permanent feature of the timetable. In 1905 it was the subject of a fictional crime mystery, 'Sir Gilbert Murrell's Picture', part of *Thrilling Stories of the Railway* by Victor Whitechurch.

Left One of the famous red London Country RF single deckers is held at the crossing gates at Colnbrook in 1976 whilst a DMU passes with an enthusiast's special working. The signal box dates from 1904 when the up platform and passing loop were brought into operation. The stationmaster's house seen behind the box was built in the same Dutch style as the main station building. The last RF was withdrawn from London Transport service in 1979.

Left The Dutch style of architecture is again apparent in this view of Colnbrook station, which closed along with the rest of the West Drayton–Staines West branch in March 1965. Freight trains continue to run to Colnbrook today, bringing in aviation fuel for Heathrow Airport and serving a local aggregates depot. Current proposals for a Western Rail Link to Heathrow envisage a route leaving the Great Western mainline between Langley and Iver via a short stretch of open railway before entering a new 5km tunnel. The tunnel would pass under Colnbrook and then join existing Underground rail lines at Heathrow Terminal 5.

MIDDLESEX

Right Staines West terminus is seen here with an oil tank wagon occupying increasingly overgrown track, reflecting traffic to the nearby Shell Mex and BP oil siding established in 1964. The arrival of the M25 motorway in 1981 severed the southern section of this branchline so a connection was laid in to the SR route to Staines enabling oil traffic to be handled until 1991. The station building was subsequently converted into office accommodation.

Right An exterior shot of the rail terminus, which also formed the start of a couple of bus routes as witnessed by the parked single-deck vehicles. A large station sign formerly occupied the site of the blank space on the white wall to the left of the station building.

LONDON

Broad Street has been one of the few London termini to close in recent years, finally shutting its doors on 30 June 1986 after a long period of declining usage. Being a prime site it was quickly demolished and replaced with the Broadgate office, shopping and restaurant complex. The formerly elegant facade had become a jumbled architectural mess by the time this picture was taken in the 1980s.

OXFORDSHIRE

Right Two views of Oxford's stations, the first featuring the signal box and signal gantry of the old run-down Great Western Railway (GWR) station which was replaced by a new structure in 1971 with further enhancements and additions in 1974 and 1990. This view looking south shows the forest of semaphore signalling then in place during the late 1960s.

Right The other station in Oxford was the LNWR's Rewley Road terminus, closed in October 1951 when services were diverted to the GWR station and seen here in use as a garage. The building was dismantled in 1999 and re-erected at the Buckinghamshire Railway's Quainton Road site.

Left Another view of Adderbury, also featured on the front cover to this volume, taken from the approach road and showing, in addition to the station buildings and signal box, the former goods shed. The area now hosts the Station Yard Industrial Estate.

Left The second Faringdon to feature in this volume, this time with only one 'r', was the terminus of a short branchline from Uffington on the GWR mainline which closed to passengers in December 1951, although freight continued until 1964. It is seen here in its unlikely second life as a chapel of rest used by a local undertaker, but today it is in use as a nursery school. Faringdon was the westernmost town in Berkshire until boundary changes saw it move to Oxfordshire in 1974.

Right Bicester's London Road station is seen here during the freight-only period of operation following closure to passengers of the Varsity Line as a through route between Oxford and Cambridge in December 1967. The development of a shopping complex near the site saw the line re-open to passengers from Oxford to a renamed Bicester Town in May 1987. The westbound platform was demolished, as were the buildings seen in this view on the remaining eastbound platform. A new chord line has been built to link into the Chiltern mainline allowing through running from Marylebone and was officially opened in October 2015, and the station renamed Bicester Village after the nearby designer retail outlet. Double track has been restored between Oxford and Bicester and a new westbound platform constructed, enabling the operation of a half hourly service between London Marylebone and Oxford via Bicester. Future extension of the route to Bletchley is envisaged and one day even Cambridge may be reached again by rail via this route.

Right The level crossing gates and station building are seen in this view of Launton. Only the westbound platform of the former station remains at this location. Launton formerly marked the boundary between the Western and Midland regions of BR.

Left Watlington's small platform and building are in danger of being engulfed in vegetation in this view. This branch from Princes Risborough was closed to passengers in 1957 and to goods in 1961. It had originally been the intention to extend the line to Wallingford, however, this was never achieved due to financial difficulties. Today the mouldering remains lie undisturbed.

Left The terminus at Blenheim & Woodstock was initially converted to a garage and petrol station after closure in February 1954 and it is in this guise that it is seen here in this 1988 view. In 2013 the land to the rear of the station building was utilised to build a small estate of high-specification houses. The station building now provides small office and commercial accommodation, with the forecourt being transformed into a small landscaped garden.

BUCKINGHAMSHIRE

Right Continuing our journey along the former Varsity line we now enter Buckinghamshire, where Claydon station, complete with buildings and level crossing gates, is seen in this view. The buildings were demolished in the 1980s and today just one platform remains. The former level crossing has now been replaced with fencing and the line here is officially classified as 'mothballed' pending any future re-opening to Bletchley and beyond. There have been recent requests for the provision of a new station for Claydon on the proposed HS2 route, which is projected to pass through the area.

Right This is the forecourt of Winslow station with its majestic trees, but sadly the station was demolished in the early 1990s and the station site redeveloped for housing. This was the second most important station on the Oxford–Bletchley route and was temporarily re-opened on Saturdays in November and December 1984 for Christmas shoppers. A single track and overgrown platforms are all that remain here today.

Unlike Loudwater, the station platform and building at Wooburn Green remained in situ as a private dwelling until the late 1980s, as the open windows and curtains testify in this view. The station was then demolished to make way for the Old Station Way development, built around 1990, and a railway conservation path, which follows the route of the former railway towards Bourne End.

The link between High Wycombe and Bourne End on the Marlow branch was a post-Beeching casualty, being severed in May 1970. The station at Loudwater was demolished and the site is now an industrial park.

HERTFORDSHIRE

Cole Green was situated on the line from Hertford to Welwyn Garden City, which closed to passengers in June 1951 and to goods in August 1962. By 1974 the roof of the station was in the ruinous state seen here and the building was demolished shortly afterwards. The site is now a car park and picnic area for the Cole Green Way and both platforms are still evident, although one is heavily overgrown.

WARWICKSHIRE

Right Washing hangs on a line beneath the canopy at Great Alne station on the former GWR line from Alcester to Bearley, which closed to passengers as early as 1917 only to reopen between 1922 and 1939. With the onset of the Second World War only workers' trains from Leamington to the nearby Maudsley Motor Works, which had relocated from war-torn Coventry, operated until 1944. The line closed completely in 1951 with lifting of the track taking place shortly afterwards, the station then becoming the local post office before assuming its current role as a residence.

Right The accommodation provided for both station staff and the crossing keeper is seen near the small wayside stop of Longdon Road on the Moreton-in-Marsh to Shipston-on-Stour branch, which closed to passengers in 1929 and to goods in May 1960. Although a pair of level crossing gates are evident in this view looking towards the small goods yard, today there is merely a hump in the road to mark the site of the crossing, the house being incorporated into a larger dwelling. One of the lines in the goods yard formerly made connection with the Stratford & Moreton wagonway.

Left A remnant of the wagonway which operated from Stratford-upon-Avon to Moreton-in-Marsh is this wooden wagon mounted on a set of rails at Stratford and seen here in the 1970s. The wagonway, which was horse drawn, ran for 16 miles from Stratford to Moreton, opening in 1826 and with a branch to Shipston-on-Stour following ten years later. In 1859 the southern section between Moreton and Shipston was converted into a proper railway. The wagonway then went bankrupt in 1868, the line being taken over by the GWR. Tracks on the northern part of the line from Shipston to Stratford, which continued to see horse-drawn traffic, were lifted in 1918. This surviving wagon was restored in 2010.

Left An architectural gem was lost when the station at Kenilworth, rebuilt in the Gothic style in 1884, was demolished. It is seen here after passenger closure came in 1965 with one freight-only line passing through and with partly demolished platforms. Some of its former grandeur remains, however, in its lofty booking hall with tiled walls and stained-glass windows surmounted by a lantern evident to the right of the footbridge. A new functional station was opened on the site in December 2017 with services running to Coventry and Leamington Spa.

NORTHAMPTONSHIRE

As featured on the rear cover to this volume this is an earlier view of Brackley Town station with rusting grass-grown tracks still in situ. In spite of an experiment from 1956 with single-unit Diesel railcars running between Buckingham and Banbury and calling additionally at two new halts which was deemed to be successful with a reported rise of 400% in passenger numbers, the service was cut back in January 1961 to operate between Buckingham and Bletchley only, until even that remaining service was withdrawn in September 1964. *Derek Fear*

Oundle's attractive station, on the line from Northampton to Peterborough, was built in the Jacobean style from local stone and closed to passengers in May 1964 and to freight in November 1972. It is seen here in the early 1980s with the building happily still retaining its tall chimneys and today it forms a handsome residence.

BIRMINGHAM

'How the mighty have fallen' might be an epitaph for this sad scene of the once important GWR Snow Hill station in the heart of Birmingham. Tracks have been removed and piles of sleepers lie awaiting collection in this view taken a few years before demolition of the whole structure. In 1972, after the last remaining shuttle services to Wolverhampton and Langley Green were withdrawn, the station became a car park for a while prior to demolition in 1977. Today cross-city rail services operate once again through a completely new modern station opened in 1987.

Above Two further views of Snow Hill looking north towards Wolverhampton and south through the tunnel mouth to Moor Street and beyond. Notice the former bookstall still in situ on the platform to the right of the tunnel entrance.

Left The mural at St Chad's Circus portrayed the history of Snow Hill in a series of mosaics by artist Kenneth Budd. A major road development started in late 2006 to replace the roundabout, seen here with a couple of West Midlands Passenger Transport Executive buses, with a traffic light-controlled junction. In the process some of the wall was demolished, the pedestrian area in the middle was infilled and the mural was not preserved.

Right Soho & Winson Green station platforms are being submerged in a sea of vegetation in this view, taken following closure of the route from Snow Hill to Wolverhampton in March 1972. Soho Benson Road tram stop now occupies the site of this former GWR station, being part of the Midland Metro light rail system which opened in May 1999.

Right Birmingham's Moor Street station is seen here whilst steam-age infrastructure, in the form of a water crane, lingers on as a DMU makes a smoky departure for stations on the North Warwickshire line. Moor Street came under threat of closure in 1969 but five local authorities objected and took the case to the High Court, which sided with the local authorities, thus preventing closure. Two new through platforms for services to and from Snow Hill – opened in 1987 and in 2002 – were given a makeover to make them a better match architecturally with the original restored station. Moor Street has increased in importance in recent years and following the re-opening of two of the original terminus platforms in 2010 is now the terminus of many Chiltern Railways services from Marylebone, as well as being an important stop for local services on the Snow Hill lines. It is the second busiest railway station in Birmingham, with 6.5 million passengers using the station in 2017/18.

LEICESTERSHIRE

Left Seen in its trackless state, this is the platform and sole remaining original building at Shenton. This was the former lamp room which now operates as the station pottery. The present station building is the reconstructed Humberstone Road station from Leicester. Note the flag flying to the left which is the standard of Richard III displaying a white boar, this monarch being the last English king to die in battle nearby in 1485.

Left and opposite Two views of Market Bosworth on the former joint Midland/ LNWR route from Nuneaton to Moira Junction near Ashby-de-la-Zouch, which closed to passengers in April 1931. There was also a branch from Shackerstone just north of Market Bosworth to Coalville which closed in 1964 to freight, although the Nuneaton–Ashby line soldiered on until 1970. These views of the station and grass-grown tracks were taken before the Battlefield Line preservation society had extended their operation from their headquarters at Shackerstone. They have subsequently extended further to Shenton near the site of the Battle of Bosworth, hence the name of the society, to give a 4 ½-mile run.

LINCOLNSHIRE

My only visit to Lincoln was by special train from Bristol in the late 1970s, the excursion terminating at St Marks station, Lincoln's first station being opened by the Midland Railway in 1846. Originally a terminus, it later became a through station via a connection to the Great Northern Railway (GNR) to the east of Lincoln Central station. Diversion of its last remaining services came in May 1985, followed by closure. The station portico has been preserved, although the remainder of the site is now a shopping centre with an original enamel station sign adorning a mock signal box, which is now the shopping centre's estate management office.

CUMBERLAND

An exterior view of Keswick's fine station building has the name displayed in ironwork above the entrance as well as a fine old red telephone kiosk to add to the interest of the scene. Unfortunately, a platform view reveals that although the platform canopy remains, the track has gone, as has the former island platform following closure, which came in March 1972. Much of the site was then used for car parking for the adjacent hotel and the main station building incorporated into the hotel, with the building being awarded Grade II listed status in 1976. Today a games room annexe to the hotel is now housed on the platform beneath the canopy. There is currently a scheme to re-open the branch from Keswick to the mainline at Penrith.

Table 169— **PENRITH, WORKINGTON AND WHITEHAVEN**

WEEKDAYS ONLY

Miles			a.m.	a.m.	a.m.	a.m.	a.m.		a.m.	p.m.	p.m.	p.m.			p.m.	p.m.	p.m.	p.m.	p.m.	p.m.	
0	**PENRITH** for Ullswater	dep.	7 18	.	9 33	.	.	.	11 38	1 32	.	.	.	.	5 0	.	6 8	.	7 45	.	.
3¼	Blencow		7⊢26	...	9 41	...	...	...	11 46	1 41	...	...	...	...	5 8	...	6 16	...	7⊢54	...	...
7¾	Penruddock		7 33	.	9 48	.	.	.	11 53	1 48	.	.	.	.	5 15	.	6 23	.	8 0	.	.
10	Troutbeck		...	...	9 53	...	...	...	11 58	1 53	...	...	...	...	5 20	...	6 28	...	...	...	...
14¾	Threlkeld		7 42	.	9 59	.	.	.	12 4	1 59	.	.	.	.	5 29	.	6 34	.	8⊢11	.	.
18¼	**Keswick**	arr.	7 48	...	10 5	...	...	...	12 10	2 5	...	...	...	...	5 35	...	6 40	...	8 17	...	...
		dep.	7 56	.	10 7	.	.	.	.	2 11	.	.	.	.	5 45	.	6 42	.	8 19	.	.
20¼	Braithwaite		7 59	...	10 10	...	...	...	...	2 14	...	...	...	...	5 48	...	6 45	...	8 22	...	...
25¼	Bassenthwaite Lake		8 5	.	10 16	.	.	.	.	2 20	.	.	.	.	5 59	.	6 51	.	8A28	.	.
30¾	Cockermouth for Buttermere	arr.	8 15	...	10 26	...	...	...	...	2 30	...	...	...	...	6 9	...	7 1	...	8 38	...	...
		dep.	8 17	.	10 26	.	.	.	.	2 30	.	.	.	.	6 12	.	7 6	.	8 40	.	.
33¼	Brigham		8 21	...	10 31	...	...	...	...	2D35	...	...	...	...	6D16	...	7D10	...	8D44	...	...
39¾	**WORKINGTON Main**	arr.	8 34	.	10 45	.	.	.	.	2 48	.	.	.	.	6 29	.	7 23	.	8 57	.	.
		dep.	.	9 17	.	10 53	11 27	...	...	...	3 12	3 24	...	...	...	7 7	...	8 17	...	9 17	...
42	Harrington		...	9 21	...	10 58	.	.	.	.	3 17	.	.	.	.	7 11	.	8 22	.	9 21	.
45	Parton		.	9 31	.	.	11 41	...	...	...	...	3 39	...	...	...	7 21	...	8 32	...	9 31	...
46¼	**WHITEHAVEN Bransty**	arr.	...	9 35	...	11 12	.	.	.	.	3 31	.	.	.	.	7 25	.	8 36	.	9 35	.

Miles			a.m.	a.m. (TC to Carlisle arr. 8.47 am.)	a.m.	a.m. (TC to Carlisle arr. 11.3 am.)	p.m.	a.m.	SX a.m.	p.m. (TC to Carlisle arr. 2.7 p.m.)	p.m.	p.m.	p.m.	SX p.m.	p.m.	p.m.	p.m.	p.m.	p.m. (TC to Carlisle arr 8.52 p.m.)
0	**WHITEHAVEN Bransty**	dep.	5 50	.	9 0	.	.	11 30	11 55	.	2 55	.	4 15	4 37	.	.	.	6 50	.
1½	Parton		5 53	...	9 3	...	...	...	11 58	...	2 58	...	4 18	...	...	...	...	6 53	...
4½	Harrington		6 3	.	9 13	.	.	.	12 8	.	3 8	..	4 28	.	.	.	6 30	.	.
6½	**WORKINGTON Main**	arr.	6 8	...	9 18	...	...	11 44	12 13	...	3 13	...	4 33	4 51	...	...	6 35	7 6	...
		dep.	...	7 5	...	9 25	...	...	...	12 25	.	3 20	...	...	5 20	...	...	...	7 15
13½	Brigham		.	7 17	.	9 37	.	.	.	12C37	.	3C33	.	.	5C33	.	.	.	7C28
15¾	Cockermouth for Buttermere	arr.	...	7 23	...	9 43	...	...	...	12 43	...	3 38	...	...	5 38	...	...	...	7 33
		dep.	.	7 25	.	9 44	.	.	.	12 44	.	3 39	.	.	5 39	.	.	.	7 33
21	Bassenthwaite Lake		...	7 34	...	9 53	...	...	...	12 54	...	3F51	...	...	5E54	...	...	...	7 43
26	Braithwaite		.	7 42	.	10 1	.	.	.	1 1	.	3 59	.	.	6 2	.	.	.	7 50
28½	**Keswick**	arr.	...	7 47	...	10 6	...	...	...	1 7	...	4 4	...	...	6 7	...	...	...	7 56
		dep.	.	7 49	.	10 7	12 42	.	.	1 9	.	4 6	.	.	.	6 55	.	.	7 56
31¾	Threlkeld		...	7 56	...	10 14	12 49	...	...	1 16	...	4 13	...	...	...	7 2	...	...	8⊢3
36¼	Troutbeck		.	8 7	.	10 25	1 0	.	.	1 27	.	4 24	.	.	.	.	.	.	...
38¾	Penruddock		...	8 12	...	10 30	1 4	...	...	1 32	...	4 29	...	...	...	7 18	...	...	8 17
42¾	Blencow		.	8 18	.	10 36	1 10	.	.	1 40	.	4 35	.	.	.	7⊢24	.	.	8⊢24
46¼	**PENRITH** for Ullswater	arr.	...	8 24	...	10 42	1 16	...	...	1 46	...	4 41	...	...	...	7 30	...	...	8 30

⊢—Stops only to set down passengers.
A—Stops at Bassenthwaite Lake only to set down passengers on notice being given to the guard at Braithwaite.
C—Stops at Brigham only to set down passengers on notice being given to the Guard at Workington Main.
D—Stops at Brigham only to set down passengers on notice being given to the Guard at Cockermouth.
E—Arrives Bassenthwaite Lake 5.49 p.m.
F—Arrives Bassenthwaite Lake 3.48 p.m.
SX—Saturdays excepted.
TC—Through Carriage.

For complete service between Workington and Whitehaven, see Table 163.

Left Seen in happier times, a green-liveried DMU has just arrived and parcels are being unloaded. The island platform is evident in the background of this August 1967 image. (Geoffrey Skelsey licensed under Wikipedia Creative Commons Attribution Share Alike 4.0 International license)

Below left Looking along the platform reveals the all too apparent changes.

Below right The line from Keswick to Cockermouth and Whitehaven was an earlier closure, occurring in April 1966, which rendered Keswick a terminus rather than a through station. This view of Bassenthwaite Lake station building taken in the early 1980s reveals that the platforms have been cut back in preparation for a road scheme which today sees traffic thundering by on the A66 close to the former station, which is now in a roofless, ruinous state. However, there are ambitious plans to restore the station, the station house, two surviving railwaymens' cottages and the one surviving platform as a cafe and holiday let. In addition a replica French Class 241P express locomotive and three coaches, used in the recent Kenneth Branagh film "Murder on the Orient Express", have recently arrived on site.

Threlkeld was an intermediate stop on the branch to Penrith and is seen here in 1979 with its unusual integral signal box situated on the island platform. Today just the platform remains. Formerly housing an eighteen-lever frame, all the signal boxes on the remaining stub of the line from Keswick closed in 1967 when the line went over to one-unit operation.

Above Two views of Troutbeck, of 'D'ye ken John Peel?' fame, with the ballast looking pretty fresh, revealing that track recovery had not long taken place. The bridge from which this late 1970s view was taken has since been demolished, as has the lofty signal box seen in the distance. The space between the platforms has been infilled to form a garden for the station, which is now a private residence.

Left Penruddock station and box are seen shortly after track removal. Very little remains on the site today to identify its railway origins.

Above Alston before and after. A view of the basic railway at Alston with a two-car DMU waiting to depart for the junction with the Newcastle–Carlisle line at Haltwhistle on 22 March 1976. The line was to close just a few weeks later, on 3 May. In its last year earnings on the branch were claimed to be just £4,000, requiring a subsidy of £77,000, and when agreement was given to the construction of an all-weather road, to prevent Alston from being cut off in bad weather, the fate of the branch was sealed.

Inset Alston terminus seen in the 1970s during the early days of preservation by the 2ft narrow gauge South Tynedale Railway, who currently operate services as far as Slaggyford. The preservation society has hopes of eventually restoring the full extent of the line to Haltwhistle.

WESTMORLAND

An exterior view of Windermere's impressive former train shed with a veteran Bedford OB coach on the 'Mountain Goat' service, which began in 1972 taking tourists and hikers to the more remote areas of the Lake District. The Bedford, known affectionately as 'Li'l Billie', was later exported to Japan to undertake a similar role transporting tourists.

Right Although reduced to single track and just one platform, the original interior of the station at Windermere is seen prior to truncation of the platforms and sale of the covered area to a retail outlet. A DMU awaits return to the mainline at Oxenholme in this 1970s view.

Right Appleby's other station was a smaller affair than that on the Settle & Carlisle route, being a stop on the cross-country Eden Valley route from Clifton Junction south of Penrith to Kirkby Stephen, where connection was made with the Darlington line. Seen here in the 1980s, the track was retained to give access to Hartley quarry and to allow the MOD to use Warcop station to load and unload vehicles for use at the nearby army camp. The army continued to use Warcop until May 1987, the line then being mothballed. The Eden Valley Railway Trust was formed in 1995 with the aim of re-opening the line between Appleby and Warcop, and they currently operate over 2.2 miles from the Warcop end. Much of the site at Appleby East has now been taken over by a scrap metal merchant.

This view of Warcop was taken in the mid-1980s during the period when the site was still used by the army, although only a single van is apparent here. Military personnel from the nearby army camp were also transported by train from the platform here. The station is in private hands and has been fenced off from the platform, whilst the preservation society use the goods yard for maintenance of their stock, much of which is stored on track to the south of the station. The signal box seen here at the end of the platform has been restored.

The once impressive station building at Kirkby Stephen East is seen here shorn of its extensive track layout and with the ends of the remaining train shed bricked in. The site had been used as a bobbin factory after closure to freight, which fortunately preserved much of the station building. There were once two train sheds separated by the central building seen here, which boasted a clock where the circular feature can now be seen. Much of the site is now an industrial estate although the Stainmore Railway Company has taken over the station with the aim of restoring it as a working railway and heritage centre set in the 1950s, the first trains running in 2011 on a short section of relaid track. There are ambitious plans to eventually link up with the Eden Valley Railway at Warcop.

When opened, Barras station was the highest mainline station in England, a title it subsequently lost to Dent. The main station building seen in this view, in front of the stationmaster's house, was dismantled in 2007 and is currently stored at Kirkby Stephen East station. The famous BTF film *Snowdrift at Bleath Gill* was set just to the north-east of this station. Note that a nameboard with its supports is still extant on the south end of the up platform by the stand of trees, no doubt planted to give some protection from the wind in this very exposed location.

NORTH WEST MOTIVE POWER DEPOTS 1968

Travelling by DMU from Manchester Victoria to Newton Heath station and then visiting Newton Heath shed (9D) in June 1968 proved to be no problem, for by that time the great number of enthusiasts found traipsing around steam sheds was largely accepted by railway staff in what were the dying days of steam. Whilst many locomotives on view were clearly unlikely to move again in revenue-earning service, there was still enough live steam, including Black 5s Nos 44890 and 45206 seen here, to provide the sights, sounds and smells of an active steam depot.

Patricroft (9F) was one of a handful of steam sheds that remained open in the summer of 1968. This panorama of the layout taken from the footbridge giving access to the shed provides a wealth of detail of the infrastructure, including the massive ferro-concrete coaling tower, associated with such a depot. The mixture of steam and diesel traction apparent here often made for a situation of 'uneasy bedfellows', where the relative cleanliness of diesel power was at variance with the grimy environment associated with steam.

Right Patricroft was known for its allocation of Caprotti Standard Class 5s and here is No 73125 representing this sub class of 4-6-0s. Inside the shed can be seen classmate No 73050, which was subsequently preserved as *City of Peterborough*, being owned by the council for that city and operated on lease by the Nene Valley Railway.

Right Standing beneath the coaling stage is Stanier (8F) No 48491 wearing a Bolton (9K) shed code.

Left Rose Grove (10F) was one of the final quartet of MPDs to remain open to steam until the end came in August 1968. Here Black 5 No 45096 rests outside the shed waiting for its next turn.

Left A view looking across the front of the shed towards the coaling stage reveals that No 45096 has been joined on shed by Standard Class 4 No 75027 which, believe it or not, was wearing green livery. In the distance is an unidentified 8F 2-8-0.

Left Approaching the turntable is No 75027, a visitor from Carnforth shed, which would go on to a life in preservation on the Bluebell Railway, arriving there in January 1969. It is flanked on the left by an unidentified Black 5 and on the right, standing by the water crane, is 8F No 48519.

Long lines of withdrawn locomotives grace the sidings at Lostock Hall (10D) depot including a couple of Ivatt 2-6-0s seen at the end of the far left siding. The massive coaling stage again dominates the skyline.

Left Seen in steam from the station platform with its vintage lamp and maroon BR totem is 8F No 48723. The loco depot eventually lost its role as a maintenance facility in 1971, thereafter taking over the role of its predecessor further east as the area carriage and wagon repair shops. It closed altogether in 1988 and was finally demolished in January 1990.

Left Streaks of rust add a much-needed splash of colour to the sombre shades of Black 5 No 44878, withdrawn at the end of July 1968 and waiting its turn to be towed away for scrap. It met its end at Cohen's scrapyard near Kettering. (See the author's book *Cohen's: A Northamptonshire Railway Graveyard* published by Crecy.)

Left I never managed to get round Bolton (9K) shed on my week's visit in 1968 and instead had to be content with a shot from a passing train. A mix of steam and diesel is apparent as is a line of modern Class 04 Drewry 0-6-0 DM diesel shunters D2227, D2234, D2226 and D2224, introduced in 1952 and, surprisingly, all withdrawn before the steam locomotives, on 13 April 1968, and scrapped at Drapers in Hull.

Above Two views of the most northerly shed to stay open to steam at Carnforth (10A). The depot continued life as Steamtown, a steam locomotive facility and museum, after closure by BR. This continued until the end of the 1987 season and although Steamtown Railway Museum Ltd still exists today as a holding company, and operates an extensive railway repair and operating facility on the site, the West Coast Railway Company Ltd is now based at the site and operates heritage steam and diesel trains across the national UK railway network.

Inset A view looking north showing the turntable and one of the preserved locomotives stored there, this being a Fairburn tank destined for the Lakeside & Haverthwaite Railway. Several withdrawn 9Fs can be seen on the far left amongst the usual diet of Black 5s and 8Fs. The red stock of the depot breakdown train is apparent on the right.

LANCASHIRE

Torver was an intermediate station on the branch from Coniston to Foxfield which closed to passengers in October 1958. Slate and stone from local quarries were important traffic at this station, which has now been converted into holiday accommodation.

Right The rusting rails and grass-grown tracks tell their own story of dereliction now that the branchline has been closed, and day-trippers will no longer arrive by train at Lakeside to take a ride on the lake steamers. The last summer season of operation was 1965, after which the line closed.

Right Resurrection came to part of the line with the opening of the preserved Lakeside & Haverthwaite Railway in 1973. Two of their steam locomotives, an LMS Fairburn tank in steam and Hudswell Clarke *Renishaw Ironworks No 6* stabled by the buffer stops, are seen under the roof girders of the terminus. Unfortunately, the roof was later removed. The industrial locomotive now resides on the Tanfield Railway.

Left Lancaster's Green Ayre shed and turntable are seen here after closure in April 1966. The line between Wennington and Morecambe via Green Ayre fell victim to the Beeching cuts and was closed to passengers on 2 January 1966, although the line through the station continued to be used for freight until 16 March 1976. The station was demolished later that year and the site of the shed is now a supermarket.

Below Preston station is still very much operational but this side, known as the East Lancs platforms, was no longer required following closure of the East Lancashire line between Preston and Bamber Bridge via its original direct route in April 1972. The East Lancs platforms – numbers 10 to 13 – were then demolished, along with the Butler Street Goods Yard, and the site covered by car parks for the station and the adjacent Fishergate Shopping Centre, built in the 1980s. In this view a loaded stone train in the capable hands of Standard Class 4 No 75027 restarts from a signal stop to round the curve into the station.

Waiting in the traditional place for assisting trains up Miles Platting bank is Black 5 No 45255. Years of accumulated soot and grime do nothing to enhance the appearance of Manchester's Victoria station.

Cautiously descending the bank comes 8F No 48319 with a train of loaded wagons. Note the railwayman walking alongside the track ready to release the wagon brakes after coming down the 1 in 47 incline.

Right Framed by the road bridge, a couple of young platform-end spotters note the passage of a Black 5 reversing into Manchester's Victoria station for its next duty.

Right Erupting from Victoria station in a volley of noise, steam and exhaust smoke, an unidentified Black 5 makes its presence felt in June 1968, epitomising the visual and audible appeal of the steam locomotive. Sadly this was a sight that would be gone from the national network within a matter of weeks.

Stanier Black 5 No 45055 waits in the parcels bay at Manchester Exchange having delivered a short van train, one of the vans being clearly chalk-marked 'Manchester'. An abundance of barrows at the platform end will doubtless come in useful to help unload the train's contents.

YORKSHIRE

Two views of a substantially intact Bowes station which, although in a decayed state, are a far cry from the few crumbling walls which are all that remain today. The date of the building's construction, 1858, can be seen over the doorway in the lower image, although the line from Barnard Castle to Tebay did not open until 1861. Complete closure came in January 1962. The signal box seen here was dismantled in 1997 for storage and eventual re-erection by the Eden Valley Railway.

A dramatically lit portrait of Bowes station reveals that many of the roof tiles are missing and that a cattle feeding trough now stands on the former trackbed.

Dent, the highest mainline station in England at 1,150 feet above sea level, witnesses the passage of a Class 47-hauled four-coach train passing through the station in 1982 during the sixteen-year period from May 1970 when it was closed to passengers. The former signal box seen in the background, closed the previous year, was subsequently demolished.

Ripon is one of the few cathedral cities in the UK to lose its railway, which occurred when the line from Leeds to Northallerton was closed to passengers in March 1967 and to freight in September 1969. Although the station building still stands, much of the route through the city is now a relief road. There is currently a campaign to re-open the line from Ripon to Harrogate at an estimated cost of £40m. This 1976 view shows both platforms, although today the former up platform is no longer extant.

Above Two 1990 images of Hawes station on the line linking the Settle & Carlisle at Garsdale, formerly Hawes Junction, with Northallerton. The route east of Hawes closed in April 1954 but it retained a link westwards to Garsdale until March 1959. After closure the site was purchased by the Yorkshire Dales National Park Authority and converted into a museum and tourist information centre in the early 1990s, in which guise it is seen here. Later embellishments have included provision of a short length of re-laid track housing a preserved industrial tank locomotive, cosmetically painted in British Railways colours, together with a pair of ex-BR Mark 1 coaches. The preserved Wensleydale Railway had plans to eventually re-open the currently abandoned and derelict section of line between Redmire and Garsdale, however, the parlous financial state of the railway has led to a rethink.

Right Aysgarth station served the nearby beauty spot of Aysgarth Falls. Although the Wensleydale Railway, once owners of the site, had long-term plans to reinstate services through here, their directors warned in 2017 that the sale of the station was crucial to the survival of the whole railway. At an AGM, supporters backed the sale alongside the new scheme to develop a 10-mile steam heritage line from Leyburn to Castle Bolton.

The quarry loading point for daily limestone trains to Redcar steelworks at Redmire station was the *raison d'être* for the continuance of freight services over the 22 miles from Northallerton after passenger closure. This traffic ceased in 1992 but the site was redeveloped in the early 1990s by the MOD to permit movement of military equipment by rail to and from the garrison at Catterick, an operation that continues periodically to this day. The Wensleydale Railway then leased the line from Railtrack and began operating heritage passenger services from Redmire in 2004 and at the time of writing they run to Leeming Bar. This view, taken during the era of limestone traffic, shows a number of freight wagons in the yard together with the loading hopper.

Right Leyburn station seen in the 1980s with signalling, passing loop and signal box still in situ. In July 2017 it was announced that the station would benefit from a grant of £72,000 allowing the re-installation of a passing loop, water tower with water cranes, a footbridge and signal box with working levers, the latter two items being donated by Network Rail from redundant assets elsewhere.

Right A 1980s view of Cloughton station, which was situated on the former Whitby–Scarborough line and which closed in March 1965. Following closure, it has been converted into a B&B establishment with tearoom and self-catering accommodation provided in an old Mk 1 coach, reflecting the former camping coach that was once based here along with others at four further sites on the route.

Left A horse and rider now occupy the former trackbed at Hayburn Wyke whose platform, still containing a pair of concrete posts for the former running in board, can be seen on the left. At the rear of the platform the original fencing is still in place, as is the stationmaster's house seen in the distance. The station was closed between March 1917 and May 1921, and became an unstaffed halt in March 1953.

Left A group of walkers are seen passing Staintondale station, which has been converted into a private residence with attractive floral displays both on the platform and on the former trackbed. The old line now forms 21 miles of Route 1 of the National Cycle Network and is very popular with both cyclists and walkers.

Right Ravenscar was very much a station for the 'town that never was'. Originally known as 'Peak' this stop on the Whitby–Scarborough line was at the summit of steep 1 in 39 climbs from both north and south. In 1895 the village of Peak was bought by a small consortium hoping to turn it into a Victorian seaside resort to rival its neighbours. Although there was some development around Station Square, the scheme failed due in large part to the fact that there was no safe and quick access to the beach some 600 feet below and to the prevalence of a dense shroud of mist that often hung about the clifftop on which the development was planned. This view shows track recovery in progress. Today parts of the unfinished development remain but the kerbstones of the unfinished streets are eerily quiet, disturbed only by strong winds off the North Sea.

Right Saplings now grow where trains once ran. The former hotel seen in the background still stands and is now Ravenscar House B&B.

Left This view of Robin Hood's Bay station shows that the main station building and stationmaster's house remain and today they continue the pattern set by the four camping coaches that were based here in BR days by providing holiday accommodation. The roof of the former platform-mounted signal box can be seen peeping over the fence. Note the circular feature to the left of the nearest window which formerly housed the station clock.

Left The grass-grown rusting tracks passing through Levisham station on the route from Malton to Grosmont via Pickering are pictured here after closure in March 1965, prior to refurbishment by the North Yorkshire Moors Railway and re-opening in 1973.

The scene at Skipton has changed considerably since this view was taken in 1994, with an electrified service to Leeds and Bradford having replaced the DMU service seen in the platform. Also long gone are the Class 37s, an example of which is seen at the head of a Carlisle service on the adjacent platform. This pair of Class 31s parked in a siding have also now vanished from the railway scene, as has the semaphore signalling. The deserted platforms numbered 5 and 6 seen on the right were added to serve the Skipton to Ilkley line and were at a slightly higher level on a rising gradient as this line ran south-west of the existing line and then crossed over it by bridge to the east. These platforms were also later used by services on the short branch to Grassington, which closed to passengers in 1930. Passenger services to Ilkley ceased in March 1965, after which platforms 5 and 6 were closed and the access subway bricked up. Whilst the line through platform 5 is still used as a single-track freight line to Swinden Quarry via the former Yorkshire Dales line, the track through platform 6 was lifted.

Left Horton-in-Ribblesdale lost its passenger service in May 1970 only to be reinstated sixteen years later in July 1986. Seen during its closure years, the signal box controls the movement of a light Class 25 locomotive held at the tall home signal. Following closure of the sidings seen in this view the box closed in 1984 and unfortunately burnt down in April 1991.

Left With the dramatic snow-covered slopes of Wild Boar Fell in the background, this view was taken from a northbound express breasting the 1,169ft summit at Ais Gill and passing the famous signal box. Following closure in May 1981 the old box has now found a new home at the Midland Railway Centre at Butterley.

The architectural gem of the line, as well as being at one time its Achilles heel, is undoubtedly Ribblehead Viaduct, seen here in its majestic landscape setting with a foreground of browsing sheep and a skyscape of scudding clouds.

Left Penistone station is now a shadow of its former importance with just branchline services from Sheffield to Huddersfield remaining. In the first view taken in 1983 looking south-east, the overhead gantries formerly supplying power to the electrified Sheffield–Manchester line remain in place. Electrification of this route was first mooted by the Great Central Railway owing to the difficulties of operating heavy steam-hauled coal trains on the Penistone–Wath section, a line with severe gradients and several tunnels. The Manchester–Sheffield–Wath electrification project was not completed until 1955, using overhead wires energised at 1,500 volts DC. By 1981 a combination of alternative available routes, an absence of passenger traffic since 1970, a downturn in cross Pennine coal traffic, plus the need to upgrade or replace the electrical locomotives and the supply system (the 25kv AC system being the preferred standard), led to the closure of the route east of Hadfield.

Left Perhaps an exhortation for 'Way Out Passengers only, man' to use the footbridge, or just an ambiguous use of words?

Left Old signage remains on the Huddersfield platform. Penistone is one of the few passing loops remaining on the branch from Barnsley.

NORTHUMBERLAND

The attractive train shed at Alnwick was the terminus for services from Cornhill, closed in September 1930, and from the East Coast Main Line (ECML) at Alnmouth, closed to passengers in January 1968. It is seen here in the 1980s during its post-closure life with loading ramps in place of platforms and with the train shed end wall bricked up. These ramps have now been replaced and the area tidied up and concreted, with part of the train shed being used by an agricultural contractor. Much of the train shed is currently in use by one of the largest second-hand bookshops in the country and although the Aln Valley Railway hopes to restore a service to Alnmouth, it will not be possible, in view of the construction of a bypass road and other commercial developments, to use the former Alnwick station so a new one on the outskirts of the town is proposed.

Left Seen in its attractive countryside setting is one of the viaducts on the Alston branch, namely that at Lambley which crosses the South Tyne river on a series of nine elegant arches. It is a Grade II listed structure and today pedestrians can access it, although it is fenced off at the Lambley end as the station here is now in private ownership.

Below left Two views of Haltwhistle, former junction of the branch to Alston. In the first view the overgrown, rusting track of the branchline can be seen curving away to the right of the departing Newcastle-bound DMU.

Below right The second image is looking west where a Carlisle-bound two-car DMU is about to depart. The tall 1901 built signal box was a feature of this junction station and although it was taken out of use in 1993, when the station was re-signalled with colour lights, it remains as office accommodation for railway staff. The track in the former Alston bay, seen on the left of the box in this view, has been subsequently lifted.

ROXBURGHSHIRE

Melrose station on the former Waverley route is seen here being slowly engulfed by vegetation. Today the A6091 Melrose bypass runs where trains once did and the right-hand side platform has been removed. In view of the success of the new Borders line from Edinburgh to Tweedbank, just a few miles distant, there are very real hopes that the new line may be extended to serve Melrose once again. The remaining station building and the fine platform canopy, which is supported by cast-iron lotus capitals, has been restored and is now a museum and restaurant.

A forlorn-looking Kelso station seen here in the mid-1970s prior to demolition. This line had probably lasted so long due to its value as a diversionary route when the ECML was blocked and indeed in the past such prestigious services as the *Flying Scotsman* had come this way on occasion. With the success of the new Borders Railway there have been calls for a reinstatement of services south of Tweedbank, not only to Carlisle but also through Kelso and on to Berwick. It remains to be seen whether Kelso will ever welcome trains back again.

Table 54

BERWICK-UPON-TWEED and KELSO

Miles		WEEKDAYS ONLY				Miles		WEEKDAYS ONLY		
		am	SO pm	SX pm	...			am	pm	
	2 Newcastle.. dep	6 55	4M40	4M25	...		St. Boswells dep	8 25	4 0	.. .. ..
	2 Edinburgh (Wav.) .. "	8G30	5 8	5 8	...					
—	BERWICK-upon-TWEED .... dep	9 56	6 33	6 37			KELSO ...... dep	8 50	4 40	.. .. ..
1¼	Tweedmouth { arr	9 59	6 36	6 40		10	Coldstream .. "	9 9	5 4	.. .. ..
	{ dep	10 6	6 43	6 47		15½	Norham ...... "	9 19	5 14	.. .. ..
7¾	Norham	10 17	6‡54	6‡58		22¼	Tweedmouth { arr	9 30	5 25	.. .. ..
13½	Coldstream	10 27	7 7	7 11			{ dep	9 37	5 34	.. .. ..
23¾	KELSO .. arr	10 43	7 24	7 28		23¾	BERWICK-upon-TWEED arr	9 40	5 37	.. .. ..
35	St. Boswells .. arr	11 8	8 0	8 0		81	2 Edinburgh arr	12D30	9F 0	.. .. ..
						90¾	2 Newcastle "	1L22	7E34	.. .. ..

For other trains between Berwick-upon-Tweed and Tweedmouth, see Table 2.

D—On Mondays to Fridays from 16th July to 24th August arrives Edinburgh 11.46 am. On Saturdays from 30th June to 18th August arrives Edinburgh 11.38 am.
E—Arrives Newcastle 7.21 pm on Fridays and Saturdays.
F—On Saturdays arrives Edinburgh 8.54 pm.
G—On Saturdays also on Monday, 6th August, departs Edinburgh 6.50 am.
L—On Saturdays arrives Newcastle 12.50 pm (11.42 am from 30th June to 28th July).
M—Connection at Tweedmouth.
SO—Saturdays only.
SX—Saturdays excepted.
‡—No staff in attendance.

A one-coach train twice a day in each direction was hardly going to be a money-spinner in the cost-conscious world of 1960s' railway operation, and thus it proved when the service between St Boswells and Berwick-upon-Tweed via Kelso was withdrawn in June 1964. In this view a BR Standard 2-6-0 of the 78XXX Class returns to Berwick with its one coach load, which proved more than ample for the handful of passengers then using the line.

Stately Leaderfoot Viaduct, also known as Drygrange Viaduct, enabled the Reston to St Boswells line to cross the River Tweed near Melrose. This railway was severely damaged by flooding during August 1948, resulting in closure of the line to passengers. Freight continued to cross the viaduct as far as Greenlaw until July 1965. Scheduled for demolition, it was upgraded to a category A listing and Historic Scotland assumed control from BR in 1996. The nineteen spans of the viaduct, which is 126ft above the river, have all been renovated.

Lonely Shankend signal box set in the rather bleak landscape of the Scottish Borders here finds a new use as a storage facility for hay bales in this view. The box was later restored as a holiday home in the 1990s. As with many of the smaller, more remote stations on the former Waverley route, which closed in January 1969, there was no appreciable population in the vicinity, the only traffic coming from isolated farms and houses. Thus any extension of the successful new Borders line from the current terminus at Tweedbank to Carlisle is unlikely to include provision of a stop at Shankend.

EDINBURGH

One might well ask where is the station? This view, taken from Telephone House in Edinburgh, shows clearly enough the famous castle perched upon its rock and the green dome of Usher Hall on the right. However, where the serried ranks of cars are now parked used to be the site of Princes Street station's platforms. This Caledonian Railway terminus was closed in September 1965 and all remaining services diverted to Waverley station. Princes Street station was demolished in 1969–70, with the city's West Approach Road being built along the trackbed in the early 1970s. The former station hotel still operates on the site and has been renamed the Waldorf Astoria Edinburgh – the Caledonian. Part of the station space still remains within the hotel and the vehicle entrance screen is still visible at the side of the hotel. The rear of the station hotel which backed onto the former station concourse can be seen on the left in this 1980s view.

PERTHSHIRE

Right Callander station plays host to preserved Caledonian 4-2-2 single No 123 with vintage carriages, seen here during the RCTS/SLS Scottish Rambler railtour of 12 April 1963. Built by Neilson & Co in 1886 as an exhibition locomotive, it was to remain in service until retirement came in 1935. Following restoration by BR, it operated a number of railtours until steam finished in Scotland. It can now be seen as a static exhibit in the Scottish Transport Museum in Glasgow. Callander was to lose its rail services following a landslide in nearby Glen Ogle in September 1965.

Right The small single-road Loch Tay shed was used by the locomotives operating the branch from Killin Junction to the station and pier at Loch Tay. Although the lakeside station closed in 1939 following withdrawal of the lake steamers, the goods siding and engine shed continued to be used. In the 1950s a hydro-electric power-generating station was built on the loch and the railway and its pier were used for bringing in materials for its construction. Although passenger services had been cut back to terminate at Killin, the track to the shed was left in place to enable locomotives to continue to come for servicing until the branch closed in September 1965 following the closure of the Callander and Oban route.

INDEX